A LITTLE BOOK ABOUT MONEY
A Pocket-Size Guide to Personal Finance

Yousell Reyes

Copyright © 2023 YRV Publishing
All rights reserved.

CONTENTS

INTRODUCTION 1

CHAPTER 1: **Understanding the Basics of Money** 6

CHAPTER 2: **Managing Your Money** 13

CHAPTER 3: **Credit and Debt** 26

CHAPTER 4: **Investing** 38

CHAPTER 5: **Building Wealth** 59

CHAPTER 6: **Protecting Your Financial Future** 71

CONCLUSION 83

ABOUT THE AUTHOR 88

INTRODUCTION

Welcome to "**A Little Book About Money**"! This book is tailored to be an easy-to-read introduction to the world of personal finance. It covers the basics of money, from what it is and its history, to managing your money, credit and debt, investing, and protecting your financial future. So, whether you're just starting your financial journey or looking to refresh your knowledge, this book will provide you with the information and tools you need to make intelligent financial decisions.

We'll explore simple and effective budgeting, saving, and investing strategies and the importance of building and maintaining good credit. We'll also discuss protecting your financial future and planning for unexpected events. By the end of this book, you'll have a solid understanding of the basics of personal finance and be on your way to achieving your financial goals.

"A Little Book About Money" is a comprehensive guide to personal finance that covers various topics essential for managing your money effectively. The book starts by introducing the basics of money, including what it is, its history, and the different forms it takes; this will provide a foundational understanding of how money works and how it has evolved.

Next, the book will explore strategies for managing your money, including budgeting, saving, and investing. These are crucial skills for achieving financial stability and reaching your financial goals. The book will also cover the basics of credit and debt, including how credit scores are determined, the different types of loans, and how to manage and pay off debt. This information is essential for building and maintaining good credit, which is vital for obtaining loans and credit cards and making significant acquisitions like home purchases.

Lastly, the book will emphasize the significance of securing your financial well-being, including having a backup fund, obtaining insurance, and drafting a will. This information is critical for ensuring that you are ready for unexpected circumstances and that your financial resources are safeguarded in case of your passing.

Overall, "A Little Book About Money" provides a comprehensive introduction to personal finance that is easy to understand and apply.

The book is designed to empower readers with the knowledge and tools they need to make sound financial decisions and achieve their financial goals.

CHAPTER 1: Understanding the Basics of Money

Money is a fundamental part of our daily life. It is utilized to buy goods and services, pay bills, etc. But what exactly is money, and how does it work? This chapter aims to shed light on the basic concepts of money, from its history to the various forms it takes and its role in our economy.

Money is defined as anything that is widely accepted in exchange for goods and services.

The history of money is long and complex, dating back to ancient civilizations. One of the earliest forms of money was bartering, where people exchanged goods and services directly without using a medium of exchange. However, as civilizations grew and trade expanded, the need for a more efficient and standardized method of exchange arose.

One of the first forms of standardized money was metal coins, which began in Ancient Greece and Rome. These coins were made of precious metals such as gold and silver, and their value was based on their weight and purity. This type of money was widely accepted and traded, making it easier for people to conduct business and trade goods.

As civilizations progressed, paper money was introduced as a form of currency. The Chinese were the first to use paper money during the Tang Dynasty in the 7th century AD. Paper money was more convenient to use and transport than metal coins and could be easily reproduced. However, it was also more susceptible to counterfeiting and inflation.

Modern money has taken many forms, including electronic cash, credit cards, and digital currencies. The history of money is ongoing, and it continues to evolve along with technological advances.

Money today is not just physical cash and coins; it also includes digital currencies, virtual money, bank transfers, and other forms of digital payments. In addition, the rise of technology and the Internet have made it possible to carry out a transaction without having to exchange cash physically; it has changed how we perceive and use money.

Cash, also known as physical currency or "FIAT," is the most common form of money. It is typically made of paper or metal and is issued by a government or central bank. Cash is widely accepted in most transactions and is easy to carry and use. However, cash can be lost or stolen and doesn't offer much security.

Credit is another form of money, but it is not physical. Instead, credit is a form of loan where a lender provides money that can be utilized to purchase goods or services. Credit is often issued through credit cards, loans, or lines of credit. Credit can help make large purchases, but it can also lead to extreme debt if not used responsibly.

Digital currency is a newer form of money, and it is becoming more and more popular. Digital currency is created, managed, and stored electronically. It is not controlled by any central authority and can be used for online transactions. Some examples of digital currencies are Bitcoin, Ethereum, and Litecoin.

Money has a long history, and it has evolved over time. Still, its purpose has always been the same: facilitating transactions and exchanging goods and services. Therefore, understanding the basics of money, its history, and its different forms is crucial for managing your money effectively and making intelligent financial decisions.

It's worth noting that money takes many forms, with cash no longer being the only option. Credit and digital currencies are gaining wider acceptance and usage. Credit, for instance, can be a convenient tool for big purchases. However, it's crucial to comprehend the details and proper use of credit to avoid financial strain and debt. Digital currencies, on the other hand, offer the convenience of online transactions. Still, it's equally important to know their potential risks and value fluctuation.

In the next chapter, we'll delve deeper into how to manage your money and budget effectively. We'll cover budgeting, saving, and investing strategies, which are crucial skills for achieving financial stability and reaching your financial goals. We'll also cover the importance of having an emergency fund and how it can protect you in case of unexpected events. So, stay tuned!

CHAPTER 2:
Managing Your Money

Effectively managing your money is crucial for attaining financial stability and reaching your financial goals. This chapter will cover different strategies for managing your money, including budgeting, saving, and investing. By understanding and implementing these strategies, you will be able to control your spending better and boost your savings.

Budgeting

Budgeting is the process of creating a plan for how to spend your money; this involves identifying your income, spending, and savings goals and determining how much capital to allocate to each category. This can be done manually or by using budget apps. The purpose of budgeting is to make sure that you spend less than you earn so that you have more freedom to save, invest, or spend on leisure. Also, this can help you achieve your financial goals, whether it is paying off debt, saving for a down payment on a house, or building an emergency fund.

The first step in budgeting is to identify how much you earn after taxes, including your salary, any bonuses, or any other sources of income. Next, you'll need to identify your expenses, including your fixed expenditures (such as rent or mortgage, utilities, and insurance) and your variable expenses (such as groceries, entertainment, and transportation). After identifying your income and expenses, you can create a plan for how to distribute your money.

Once you know how much money you have left over after paying your weekly, bi-weekly, or monthly obligations, you should wisely allocate that remaining money to various purposes based on your goals and financial needs. For example, you could set aside a certain percentage of that income for savings, another part to pay off debt, and another percentage for discretionary spending. Budgeting apps and online tools can help you stay organized on all of the above, so be sure to look for the one that fits your needs.

Remember, the main objective of budgeting is to help you manage your income and expenses in a way that allows you to reach your financial goals. By creating a budget and following it closely, you can control your spending and ensure that you put enough money into savings, debt repayment, and investment; this will help you make the most of your income and secure a better financial future.

It is important to note that budgeting is an ongoing process. You may need to adjust your budget as your income and expenses change over time. For example, if you get a raise or a new job, you'll need to adjust your budget accordingly. Similarly, if your expenses increase, you'll need to adjust your budget to reflect these changes.

Saving

Saving is the practice of setting aside a portion of your money for future expenses, emergencies, or investments. It is essential to save for unexpected events, such as a medical emergency or job loss, as well as for long-term goals, such as retirement or buying a home.

Saving is essential to managing your money effectively and achieving your financial goals.

It is highly recommended that you have an emergency fund, a savings account set aside expressly for unexpected expenses, such as car repairs, medical bills, or job loss. Additionally, it is advised to have at least **three to six months** of living expenses to be prepared for unplanned events.

For long-term goals, such as retirement or buying a home, it is crucial to start saving early and consistently. The earlier you start saving, the more time your money has to grow, and the more you accumulate over time.

One common strategy for saving is to set up automatic transfers from your checking account to a savings account. This can be done at set intervals, such as every pay period or when you receive a bonus. By automating your savings, you can ensure that a portion of your income is going towards your savings goals, making it less likely that you will spend it.

Another strategy for saving is to use the Envelope method, which involves allocating a set amount of cash for specific expenses and placing the cash in designated envelopes; this can help you stay within your budget and be more mindful of your spending, as you can physically see the money you have left for each category. This method can help you avoid overspending and increase your savings.

Investing

Investing is the process of using your money to make more money. It can be a great way to build wealth over time, but it does come with risks. Investing can take many forms, including stocks, bonds, mutual funds, Real Estate, etc. Each type of investment has its own set of risks and potential returns, so it is important to research and understand the different types of assets, including their pros, cons, etc., before putting your money into any of those.

Stocks, also known as equity, are a type of investment representing a company's ownership. When you buy a stock, you buy a small part of the company and become a shareholder. Keep in mind that investing in stocks can be risky as the value of shares can fluctuate based on the company's performance, market conditions, and the economy as a whole.

On the other hand, bonds are a type of investment in which an investor loans money to a company or government for a fixed period. In return, the borrower promises to pay interest to the investor and to return the original investment at the end of the term. Bonds are considered less risky than stocks but typically have lower returns.

Real Estate is another popular form of investment. It involves purchasing property to rent or resell for a profit. Real Estate can be a fantastic way to build wealth over time. Still, it does come with risks, such as market fluctuations, changes in interest rates, and the overall economy.

Mutual funds are a type of investment that pools money from many investors to buy a diversified portfolio of stocks, bonds, or other securities. They are professionally managed and provide investors with a way to diversify their portfolios without buying individual stocks or bonds.

When considering investing, it is necessary to understand the risks associated with each type of investment and to diversify your portfolio. A diversified portfolio means spreading your investment across different types of assets and industries, which will help you reduce the risk of losing all your money if a single investment performs poorly. Like always, you must research and understand the different types of investments before putting your money into any investment.

Credit Score

Managing your money effectively also includes monitoring your credit score. A credit score is a numerical representation of your creditworthiness. Lenders use it to determine your ability to repay a loan or credit card debt. Therefore, you must maintain a good credit score to obtain loans and credit cards and qualify for better interest rates.

Your credit score is determined by various factors, including your payment history, credit utilization, length of credit history, and the types of credit you have. One of the most critical factors is your payment history, which includes whether you pay your bills on time. Late payments can negatively impact your credit score, making it more difficult to obtain loans and credit cards.

Another important factor is credit utilization, which is the amount of credit you use in relation to your credit limit. It is important to keep your credit utilization low, which means using less than 30% of your available credit. High credit utilization can hurt your credit score, and lenders may see it as a sign that you're overextending yourself financially.

To maintain a good credit score, it is also essential to keep your credit card balances low. High credit card balances can indicate to lenders that you are living beyond your means, which may decrease your credit score. Additionally, applying for too many new credit cards or loans can negatively impact your credit score, as it may indicate that you are having financial difficulties.

It is crucial to frequently check your credit report to ensure that all the information it holds is accurate. This way, you can identify potential fraudulent activities, safeguard your financial future, and maintain a good credit score. You can request a free credit report from the three major credit bureaus once a year and sign up for credit monitoring services that will notify you of any changes or suspicious activity on your credit report.

Another way to safeguard your finances is to exercise caution when sharing personal information like social security numbers or credit card details. For example, be cautious of unsolicited phone calls or emails that request such information, and only provide personal data if you initiated the communication yourself.

In summary, managing your money requires budgeting, saving, investing (wisely), monitoring your credit score, and protecting yourself from fraud and scams. By understanding and implementing these strategies, you'll be able to control your spending better and increase your savings, allowing you to achieve your financial goals.

In the next chapter, we will discuss the basics of credit and debt and how to manage them.

CHAPTER 3:
Credit and Debt

Credit and debt are integral parts of our financial lives, and understanding how they work is crucial for making wise financial decisions. This chapter will explore the basics of credit and debt, including how credit works, how to manage debt, and how to avoid common mistakes.

Credit

Credit is a financial tool that allows individuals to borrow money to purchase goods or services. It is often issued in the form of credit cards, loans, or lines of credit. When you use credit, you are borrowing money you will need to pay back, usually with interest. Interest is the cost of borrowing money, typically expressed as a percentage of the borrowed amount.

Credit cards are one of the most common forms of credit; they allow you to borrow a certain amount of money, up to a credit limit and use it to make purchases. Of course, you will need to repay the amount borrowed and any interest and fees that may apply.

Loans are another form of credit. They are typically needed for large purchases, such as buying a car, a house or consolidating debt. They usually have a fixed interest rate, a fixed repayment term, and an amount to be paid back.

A line of credit is a flexible form of credit; it allows you to borrow up to a specified limit, as needed, and repay as much as you can every month. The interest rate is usually adjustable and may change based on market conditions.

Credit can be a helpful tool for making large purchases, such as a car or a house, and consolidating debt. Still, it is important to use it responsibly to avoid debt. Misusing credit can lead to high levels of debt, which can cause financial stress and make it challenging to achieve your financial goals.

Taking advantage of credit requires a good credit score, a numerical representation of your creditworthiness. Lenders use it to determine your ability to pay off a loan or credit card debt. A good credit score indicates that you are a responsible borrower and are more likely to pay your debts on time. On the other hand, a low credit score can demonstrate a history of late payments or high levels of debt, making it difficult to obtain credit in the future.

To maintain a good credit score, paying your bills on time, keeping your credit card balances low, and monitoring your credit report for suspicious activity is a must. Factors such as missed payments, high credit card balances, and negative information on your credit report can negatively impact your credit score.

In summary, using credit responsibly can have several benefits in building wealth. Some of these benefits include:

1. Building credit history: Using credit and making payments on time can help build a positive credit history, which can make it easier to get approved for loans and credit in the future.
2. Access to credit: Credit can be useful for making large purchases, such as buying a home or a car, which can be challenging to do with cash alone.

3. Building wealth through credit card rewards: Some credit cards offer rewards, such as cashback or travel points, for using the card; this can be a way to earn extra money while building wealth.
4. Leveraging credit to invest: By using credit to invest in assets such as Real Estate or stocks, you can potentially earn a higher return on investment than if you were to invest only with cash.
5. Building an emergency fund: By having a line of credit, you can use it in emergencies instead of dipping into your savings.

It is crucial to use credit in a thoughtful and controlled manner. Excessive debt and missed payments can negatively affect your credit score and overall financial health.

Debt

Debt is the amount of money that you owe to creditors. It can come in many forms, such as credit card debt, student loan, or mortgage debt. Each type of debt has its pros and cons, and it is important to understand the differences between them to make informed financial decisions.

Credit card debt, for example, is considered "bad debt" because it is often used to purchase items that lose value quickly, such as clothes or electronics. In addition, the interest rates on credit cards are usually high, making it difficult to pay off the debt promptly.

On the other hand, mortgage debt is considered "good debt" because it allows you to purchase an asset, such as a house. In addition, the interest rates on mortgages are typically lower than credit card debt, and the interest paid on a mortgage may be tax-deductible.

Student loan debt is a form of debt that can be considered both good and bad; it can be regarded as good because it allows individuals to invest in their education, leading to better job opportunities and higher earnings. However, the high-interest rates and long-term repayment schedule can also be considered bad.

Managing debt effectively involves creating a plan to pay off your debts, starting with the highest interest debt.

High-interest debt, such as credit card debt, should be a priority to pay off because it will cost you more in interest charges over time. It is also important to create a budget and stick to it, so you can avoid taking on new debt while trying to pay off existing debt.

Consolidating debt can also be a useful strategy; this means taking out one loan to pay off multiple debts. It can help simplify your payments and may also help you secure a lower interest rate. Again, this can be a great way to simplify your monthly payments and make it easier to pay off your debt.

One common mistake people make when dealing with debt is only making the minimum payments on their credit cards; this can lead to paying more interest and taking longer to pay off the debt. It is highly advised to pay more than the minimum, if possible, to reduce the interest you'll pay over time.

Another mistake is taking on too much debt at once, for example, applying for multiple credit cards or loans simultaneously; this can lower your credit score, making it more challenging to obtain new credit. Therefore, you must be mindful of how much debt you are taking on and avoid taking on more than you can handle.

It is also important to be aware of scams, such as companies offering to settle or consolidate your debt for a fee. Be wary of any company that asks for money upfront before they have done any work to help you manage your debt.

Seven tips to help you manage your debt:

1. Create a budget: This will help you understand where your money is going and where you can cut back on expenses to put more towards paying off your debt.

2. Prioritize your debt: Focus on paying off the debt with the highest interest rate first, as it will cost you more in the long run.
3. Make more than the minimum payment: Paying more than the minimum will help you pay off your debt faster.
4. Consider a debt consolidation loan: If you have multiple high-interest debts, a consolidation loan can help simplify your payments and lower the overall interest rate on your debt.
5. Negotiate with creditors: If you're having trouble making your payments, reach out to your creditors and see if they can work out a payment plan or offer a lower interest rate.
6. Avoid taking on new debt: As you work on paying off your existing debt, avoid taking on new debt; this will make it harder

to get out of debt and could prolong the process.
7. Seek professional help: If you're overwhelmed by your debt, consider seeking help from a financial advisor or credit counselor. They can help you develop a debt repayment plan and offer additional resources and support.

In summary, credit and debt are integral to our financial lives, and understanding how they work is crucial for making wise financial decisions; using credit responsibly, maintaining a good credit score, and creating a plan to pay off debt, starting with the highest-interest debt first. It is also important to be aware of scams and to avoid taking on too much debt at once. By effectively understanding and managing credit and debt, you can achieve financial stability and reach your financial goals.

CHAPTER 4:
Investing

Building wealth over time requires a strategic approach to investing. Instead of keeping your money in a savings account, investing it can yield higher returns. However, it is essential to be aware of the potential risks involved with different types of investments before deciding. Understanding the various options available is crucial for making informed investment choices.

<u>Stocks</u>

The stock market is a marketplace where publicly traded companies' stocks are bought and sold; this is one of the most popular forms of investing. When you invest in stocks, you buy a piece of ownership in a publicly traded company, meaning you own a small portion of the company. As a result, the value of your investment can go up or down depending on the performance of the company and the overall stock market.

A company's performance is measured by various financial metrics such as revenue, earnings per share, and return on equity. A company performing well and generating consistent profits is more likely to see its stock price increase. On the other hand, a company that is not performing well or is facing financial difficulties is more likely to see its stock price decrease.

The overall stock market is also important in determining your stock investment's value. The stock market is affected by numerous factors, such as economic conditions, interest rates, and political events. For example, a strong economy and low-interest rates tend to be good (bullish) for the stock market. In contrast, a weak economy and high-interest rates tend to be bad (bearish).

Stocks are considered high-risk investments because the value of your investment can be affected by both the performance of the company and the overall stock market. As a result, the value of your investment can go up or down, and there is no guarantee that you will earn a return on your investment. However, stocks also have the potential for high returns. Over the long term, the stock market has historically generated positive returns.

It is important to remember that investing in stocks is not a short-term strategy and to be patient because even the most successful companies may have periods of poor performance. It is also a good practice to diversify your investments, meaning to invest in different stocks and sectors so that if one stock or sector underperforms, it will not significantly impact your portfolio, unless the overall economy is also affected.

Investing in stocks can give you a stake in the ownership of a publicly traded company, with the potential for high returns. However, it is essential to keep in mind that stock prices can be affected by the performance of the company and the overall market, making it a high-risk investment. Therefore, it is recommended to diversify your portfolio, research, and have a long-term investment perspective to maximize your chances of success.

Bonds

Bonds are another type of investment. When you invest in bonds, you essentially lend money to a government or a corporation. They promise to pay you interest and return your original investment at the end of the bond's term. Bonds are considered less risky than stocks but generally have lower returns.

Bonds are a type of debt security that governments, municipalities, and corporations issue to raise capital. When you invest in bonds, you essentially lend money to the issuer in exchange for regular interest payments and the return of your principal at the bond's maturity date.

The bond issuer, such as a government or corporation, is responsible for paying the bondholder a specified interest rate, known as the coupon rate, at regular intervals, usually every six months. At the end of the bond's term, also known as the maturity date, the issuer will return the bondholder's principal investment.

The return on bonds is determined by the coupon rate and the bond's price at the time of purchase. The return will be higher if the bond is purchased at a discount to its face value.

The issuer's creditworthiness also plays a vital role in determining the risk of a bond investment. For example, bonds issued by the government or well-established companies are considered less risky than bonds issued by newer or less financially stable companies.

It is important to note that bond prices can fluctuate, and the value of your bond investment may be affected by changes in interest rates. When interest rates rise, bond prices fall, and when interest rates fall, bond prices rise; this means that bond investments may not be suitable for short-term investment goals.

In summary, bonds are a type of debt security that governments, municipalities, and corporations issue to raise capital. When you invest in bonds, you essentially lend money to the issuer in exchange for regular interest payments and the return of your principal at the bond's maturity date. Bonds are considered less risky than stocks because they provide a fixed income stream and a guarantee of the return of principal at maturity, but they also generally have lower returns. The issuer's creditworthiness and interest rates also play an important role in determining the risk of a bond investment.

Real Estate

Investing in Real Estate can be a terrific way to generate income and grow wealth over time. For example, you can earn a steady income from rental payments by purchasing property and renting it out. Additionally, if the property's value increases over time, you can sell it for a profit. Real Estate is an excellent option for those looking for a more tangible asset, as opposed to stocks or bonds, which may be considered more abstract. Real Estate investments include residential properties, commercial properties, and land.

When you invest in Real Estate, you buy a property intending to rent or resell it for a profit. Rental income can provide a steady stream of cash flow, and the appreciation of the property value over time can provide a substantial return on investment.

However, Real Estate investments also come with risks. For example, the value of a property can be affected by changes in the Real Estate market, such as changes in the economy, interest rates, and the local housing market; this can impact the property's value, making it difficult to sell or refinance. In addition, property ownership comes with costs such as taxes, insurance, and maintenance.

It is highly recommended that you research and understand the local Real Estate market and the specific property you are interested in investing in. It is also important to have a clear investment strategy, whether it is to generate cash flow through rental income or to generate long-term capital appreciation.

Real Estate investment trusts (REITs) are another way people can invest in income-producing Real Estate without purchasing and managing physical property. REITs are companies that own, operate, or finance a portfolio of properties, such as apartments, office buildings, shopping malls, and more. By investing in a REIT, individuals can gain exposure to the Real Estate market and receive a steady stream of income through dividends from the rental income generated by the properties in the REITs portfolio. In addition, REITs also have the potential for capital appreciation as the value of properties in the portfolio increases.

REITs can also provide diversification for an investment portfolio and are publicly traded, making it easy to buy and sell. However, it is essential to note that REITs, like any other investment, carry risks and should be researched and understood before investing in them.

In short, Real Estate is a popular form of investment that can provide a steady stream of income through rental income or capital appreciation when the property sells for a higher price than it was paid for. Real Estate investments can be profitable, but they also come with risks, such as changes in the Real Estate market, the costs of maintaining the property, and the possibility of not finding tenants. Real Estate investments can also be made through REITs, which allows investors to participate in the ownership of a diversified portfolio of properties without the need for a substantial investment or the responsibilities of being a landlord.

It is essential to do your research, understand the local Real Estate market and the specific property you are interested in, and have a clear investment strategy, whether to generate cash flow through rental income or long-term capital appreciation. It is also essential to have a solid plan in place for managing the property and dealing with any unexpected expenses.

Mutual Funds & ETFs

Investing in mutual funds and exchange-traded funds (ETFs) is another way to invest in the stock market and diversify your portfolio.

Mutual funds and ETFs are pools of money from many investors that professional money managers manage. Mutual funds are a professionally managed investment vehicle that pools money from many investors to purchase a diversified portfolio of stocks, bonds, or other securities. Mutual funds are typically managed by professional money managers who make investment decisions on behalf of the fund's shareholders. They come in different types, such as equity funds, bond funds, and money market funds, each with different investment objectives.

ETFs are similar to mutual funds in that they expose investors to a diversified portfolio of stocks, bonds, or other securities. The main difference is that ETFs are traded like stocks on an exchange, while mutual funds are bought and sold at the end of the trading day at the net asset value (NAV) price. ETFs also have lower expense ratios than mutual funds, which means they are cheaper to own.

Diversification is one of the main advantages of investing in mutual funds and ETFs. By investing in a pool of stocks, bonds, or other securities, investors can spread the risk of their investments across multiple assets, which can help reduce the portfolio's overall risk.

Additionally, mutual funds and ETFs are managed by professional money managers who are experienced in the markets and can make smart investment decisions on behalf of investors.

It is important to note that mutual funds and ETFs still carry some risk. Their performance may be affected by the execution of the underlying securities in the fund, as well as the skill of the money manager. Therefore, it is important to research and understand the fund's investment objective, the securities it holds, its historical performance, and its associated fees before deciding to invest.

In summary, investing in mutual funds and ETFs is another way to invest in the stock market and diversify your portfolio. They are pools of money from many investors that are managed by professional money managers, who use the pooled funds to buy a diversified portfolio of stocks, bonds, or other securities. As a result, mutual funds and ETFs can provide a diversified portfolio with less risk than investing in individual stocks.

It is important to remember that no investment is risk-free, and it is necessary to do your research and understand the different types of investments before putting your money into any kind of asset. **Having a well-structured investment plan and spreading your investments across various options is crucial in mitigating risk and maximizing returns.**

Investing and building wealth is vital to achieving financial stability and reaching your financial goals. It is important to understand the different types of investments. To have a clear investment plan, diversify your investments to minimize risk. It is also essential to have a financial plan, which includes creating a budget, saving for retirement, and planning for unexpected expenses. A financial planner can help you create a plan tailored to your specific needs and goals.

Building wealth is a marathon, not a sprint, and it requires persistence, self-control, and consistency. It is crucial to consistently monitor and modify your investment portfolio and financial strategy as your life evolves. To end this chapter, let's discuss some practical tips for investing.

Ten tips on investing

1. Start by setting clear investment goals. What do you want to achieve through investing? Is it long-term growth, income, or a

combination of both? Having clear goals will help you make better investment decisions.
2. Diversify your investments. Don't put all your eggs in one basket. Instead, spread your money across different asset classes, such as stocks, bonds, Real Estate, and cash; this will help reduce the risk of losing your entire investment if one asset class performs poorly.
3. Understand the risks involved. Every investment comes with its own set of risks. Make sure you are comfortable with the level of risk involved before investing.
4. Learn about the several types of investments. Do your research on different assets and understand how they work; this will help you make informed decisions about where to put your money.

5. Invest in what you know. It is easier to make informed decisions when you understand the industry or sector you're investing in.
6. Have a long-term perspective. Investing is a long-term game. So do not get caught up in short-term market fluctuations. Instead, focus on your long-term goals and invest for the long haul.
7. Keep an eye on fees. High fees can eat into your returns, so make sure you understand the fees associated with any investment and factor them into your decision-making.
8. Be patient. Building wealth takes time. Don't get discouraged if you don't see immediate returns. Stay the course and stay invested for the long term.
9. Keep an eye on taxes. Understand the tax implications of your

investments and consider them when making investment decisions.
10. Have a plan for selling your investments. When it is time to sell your investments, have a plan to ensure you do not sell at the wrong time and miss out on potential returns.

Investing and building wealth is crucial to achieving financial stability and reaching your financial goals. It is important to understand the different types of investments, have a clear investment plan, diversify your investments, and review and adjust your investment portfolio and financial plan as your life circumstances change. Taking advantage of tax-advantaged savings plans and increasing your income can also help you build wealth. Finally, remember that building wealth is a long-term process that requires patience, discipline, and consistency.

CHAPTER 5:
Building Wealth

Building wealth is a long-term process that requires patience, discipline, and a sound investment strategy. It is not something that can be achieved overnight; it is a journey that requires time, dedication, and a solid plan. It is crucial to understand that there's no universal approach to building wealth and that the best strategy for you will vary depending on your situation, objectives, and risk appetite. With that in mind, here are ten tips that can help you on your journey to building wealth:

Start early

Starting early is vital to building wealth because it allows your money to compound over time. The power of compounding means that your returns generate returns, leading to exponential growth. The longer your money is invested, the more it can grow, providing you with a larger nest egg in the long run. Additionally, starting early allows you to take on more risk because you have more time to ride out market fluctuations and recoup any losses. Even small contributions made consistently over time can add to a significant sum. So, if you haven't started investing, don't delay any longer. The earlier you start, the better off you'll be in the long run.

Create a budget

As mentioned in previous chapters, creating a budget is crucial in building wealth. It allows you to clearly understand your income and expenses, which helps you identify areas where you can cut back on spending and redirect that money toward investments. Having a budget can also help you prioritize your expenses, so you can focus on the most important things. It can also help you track your progress toward your financial goals and make adjustments as necessary. Additionally, setting a budget can help you avoid overspending and going into debt, which can negatively impact your credit score and overall financial well-being. With a budget in place, you can control your finances and ensure that your money works for you to help you reach your financial goals.

Pay off high-interest debt

Paying off high-interest debt, such as credit card debt, is key to building wealth. The interest rates on credit card debt can be extremely high, and paying only the minimum balance can cause the debt to linger for years. By paying off high-interest debt, you could free up money that can be invested to grow your wealth. Additionally, reducing or eliminating high-interest debt can also improve your credit score, which can open up new opportunities for borrowing at lower interest rates in the future. Furthermore, not having to worry about high-interest debt payments can also help to reduce stress and increase your financial peace of mind, which can help you to stay focused on your long-term wealth-building goals.

Invest in a diverse range of assets

Diversifying your investments across different asset classes can also help you build wealth by taking advantage of varying market conditions and opportunities. For example, suppose the stock market is underperforming. In that case, other asset classes, such as bonds or Real Estate, may still present a promising investment opportunity. Moreover, this strategy can help balance losses in one asset class with gains in another. It is also important to note that diversifying your investments does not guarantee a profit or protect against loss. Still, it can help reduce the impact of market volatility on your portfolio.

Take advantage of tax-advantaged accounts

Investing in tax-advantaged accounts, such as 401(k)s and IRAs, can be a smart way to save on taxes and build your wealth simultaneously. These accounts allow you to make contributions that can lower your taxable income and grow your savings over time. In addition, many 401(k) plans offer employer-matching contributions, which can boost your savings. However, it is important to note that there are limits to the amount you can contribute to these accounts each year, and you may face penalties for over-contributing. Therefore, you should consult a financial advisor or tax professional for more information on how these accounts can benefit your financial situation.

Stay invested for the long-term

Investing is a long-term strategy; trying to time the market or constantly switching investments can be detrimental to your wealth-building efforts. Instead, it is important to have a well-diversified portfolio and to stick to your investment plan, even during market downturns; this can help you to avoid making emotional decisions based on short-term market fluctuations and to stay focused on your long-term financial goals. It is also important to remember that investing in individual stocks can be riskier than investing in a diversified stock market index fund.

Keep your expenses low

Keeping your expenses low can help you to save more money to invest. By cutting back on unnecessary expenses and finding ways to save money, you can free up money that can be invested to grow your wealth; this can include finding ways to reduce housing costs, cutting back on entertainment expenses, and being strategic about transportation expenses. Additionally, small savings on daily expenses such as food and shopping can add up over time. It is essential to strike a balance between living in the present and saving for the future. By being mindful of your expenses, you can make more money available for investing, which can help you to achieve your long-term financial goals.

Invest in yourself

Investing in yourself, such as through education or training, can help you increase your earning potential and grow your wealth; this can include continuing your education, taking professional development courses, or learning a new skill. Investing in yourself can increase your earning potential and create more opportunities for growth and success in your career, which can ultimately help you grow your wealth over time. Additionally, it is important to have a long-term career plan and continuously upgrade yourself to align with the industry's current trends and demands; this will keep you relevant and valuable in the job market.

Furthermore, developing new skills or knowledge can also help you be more valuable in your current role, leading to promotions or bonuses. In addition to increasing your earning potential, investing in yourself can also help you be more confident and have a better sense of self-worth, which can positively impact your overall well-being. Overall, investing in yourself is a valuable way to grow your wealth and improve your quality of life.

Take calculated risks

Building wealth requires making strategic investment decisions, which often includes taking on some risk. However, taking calculated risks, rather than blindly jumping into investments, can increase returns and help grow your wealth over time. To do this effectively, it is essential to understand any investment's potential risks and rewards before deciding. Diversifying your investments across different asset classes and sectors can help to spread the risk and reduce the impact of any potential losses. Additionally, it is important to have a well-defined investment strategy, understand your risk tolerance, and revisit your portfolio periodically to ensure that it aligns with your goals and objectives.

Seek professional advice

Building wealth can be complicated, and seeking professional advice is important if you're unsure about any aspect of your investment strategy. A financial advisor can provide valuable guidance and expertise in asset allocation, portfolio diversification, tax planning, and retirement planning. They can also help you understand the different types of investments available and how they can help you achieve your financial goals. Additionally, they can provide ongoing support and advice as your circumstances and plans change. They can also help you stay on track and adjust your investment strategy as needed. It is important to note that working with a financial advisor is not a one-time event but rather an ongoing relationship that can help you achieve your long-term financial goals. Therefore, it is always recommended to do your due diligence when selecting a financial advisor to ensure they are a good fit for you and your financial needs.

Building wealth is a long-term process that requires patience, discipline, and a sound investment strategy. Following these tips can boost your chances of success and increase your wealth over time.

Remember, the key to building wealth is to start early, stay invested long-term, and take calculated risks.

CHAPTER 6:
Protecting Your Financial Future

To protect your financial well-being, it is crucial to take proactive measures to safeguard it. This section will discuss various tactics for securing your financial future, such as establishing emergency savings, obtaining insurance coverage, and preparing for retirement.

Emergency fund

The main benefit of having an emergency fund is that it can keep you from getting into debt or relying on high-interest credit cards in an emergency. An emergency fund can also allow you the financial flexibility to take advantage of unexpected opportunities, such as investing in a new business or a new job that may require relocation. Therefore, building an emergency fund should be a priority. It would be best if you made regular contributions, such as setting up automatic transfers from your checking account to your savings account. Another way to build an emergency fund is to look for ways to cut expenses and redirect savings into your emergency fund.

Having quick access to the funds when needed is essential. Still, it would be best to keep them in a place where they're not easily accessible, so you're less likely to spend them on non-emergency expenses. An emergency fund can prepare you for unexpected events and protect your financial future.

Insurance

Securing insurance coverage is another crucial aspect of protecting your financial future. There are different types of insurance, such as health, life, and property. These types of insurance can protect you and your assets in case of unexpected events. Having the right coverage can provide peace of mind knowing that you and your loved ones will be taken care of in case of unforeseen circumstances. For instance, health insurance can assist in paying for medical expenses, preventing large medical bills from causing financial stress. Likewise, life insurance can provide financial assistance to your loved ones in case of your death, ensuring they can maintain their standard of living and cover expenses like funeral costs. Finally, property insurance can secure your home and other assets from damage or loss due to natural disasters or other events. Therefore, it is essential to understand the different types of insurance available and to have the right coverage to protect yourself and your assets.

Alongside common forms of insurance, there are also specialized options like disability insurance, which can provide financial assistance in the event of an injury or illness that prevents you from working, and long-term care insurance, which can help cover ongoing care expenses for chronic conditions or disabilities.

One of the most valuable types of life insurance is the **Indexed Universal Life Insurance** or **IUL**, a type of permanent life insurance that provides both death benefit protection and a cash value component. The cash value component is usually invested in a variety of indexed accounts, which are linked to a stock market index, such as the S&P 500; this allows policyholders to earn a return on their cash value that is tied to the performance of the underlying index while also having a guaranteed minimum interest rate.

One of the main benefits of IUL is that it offers the potential for higher returns on the cash value component compared to traditional whole-life insurance policies. Additionally, IUL policies typically have flexible premium payments and death benefit options, allowing policyholders to adjust their coverage as their needs change over time. IUL policies also offer tax-deferred growth on the cash value component, which can help to accumulate wealth over time. IUL policies also provide the policyholder with a death benefit even if the cash value component is zero, which can provide the policyholder with peace of mind knowing that the policyholder's loved ones will be taken care of in case of death.

It is necessary to review your insurance coverage regularly, as your needs may change over time. For instance, you may need to increase your life insurance coverage if you have a growing family. It is also important to shop around and compare insurance policies from different providers to find the best coverage at the most affordable price.

It is crucial to seek guidance from an insurance expert to evaluate the options available and determine which coverage best suits your needs. They can assist in deciphering policy details and ensure you get the most favorable value for your money. Remember, by having the appropriate insurance coverage, you can safeguard your financial future and guarantee that you and your family are protected in case of unforeseen occurrences.

Planning for retirement

Planning for retirement is also an essential step in protecting your financial future. Retirement planning involves setting goals and creating a plan for achieving them. This includes understanding the different types of retirement accounts available, such as 401(k)s and IRAs, and determining how much you need to save to achieve your retirement goals. It is important to start saving for retirement as early as possible to take advantage of the power of compound interest and to ensure that you have enough money to support yourself during your retirement years.

Retirement planning is critical to ensuring that you are financially secure in your later years. Therefore, it is crucial to start thinking about retirement early on in your career and develop a plan to help you achieve your retirement goals. This means understanding the different types of retirement accounts available, such as 401(k)s, IRAs, and Roth IRAs, and determining the best fit for you based on your current financial situation and future goals. It is also essential to understand the tax implications of different retirement accounts and to take advantage of any employer-matching contributions or other incentives.

Another important aspect of retirement planning is determining how much you need to save to achieve your retirement goals; this will depend on factors such as your expected retirement age, desired lifestyle during retirement, and the cost of living in your area. A financial advisor can help you determine how much you need to save to achieve your retirement goals and create a plan to help you achieve them.

Retirement planning also includes evaluating your risk tolerance and balancing it with your investment strategy. Remember to have a diversified portfolio and ensure that your investments align with your risk tolerance and retirement goals. It is always recommended to consult a financial advisor to help you create a comprehensive retirement plan that considers your individual circumstances, objectives, and risk tolerance.

In summary, planning for retirement is a crucial aspect of protecting your financial future. It is essential to start thinking about it early on, understand the different types of retirement accounts available, determine how much you need to save to achieve your retirement goals, and ensure that your investments align with your risk tolerance and retirement goals. A financial advisor can be a valuable resource in helping you to create a comprehensive retirement plan.

In conclusion, protecting your financial future should be at the top of your list. By creating an emergency fund, buying insurance, and planning for retirement, you can ensure that you are prepared for unexpected events and have the resources you need to support yourself and your loved ones. You must understand the different types of insurance and retirement accounts available and create a plan that works for you. Additionally, you should regularly review and adjust your plan as your circumstances change. This may include increasing your contributions to your emergency fund or retirement accounts, re-evaluating your insurance coverage, and reassessing your financial goals. It is also essential to seek professional advice from a financial advisor if you need clarification on any aspect of your investment strategy. A financial advisor can help you create a comprehensive plan that considers your circumstances, goals, and risk tolerance. Furthermore, staying informed and educated about the different financial options available to you is always important and staying on top of any changes in tax laws and regulations that may affect your financial plan. By taking a proactive approach to protecting your financial future, you can ensure that you are prepared for any unexpected events and have the resources you need to support yourself and your loved ones during your retirement years.

CONCLUSION

In conclusion, this book has provided an overview of the basics of money, including understanding how money works, managing your money, credit and debt, investing and building wealth, and protecting your financial future. We have discussed key concepts such as budgeting, saving, and investing, as well as the different forms of investments such as stocks, bonds, Real Estate, and cryptocurrency. We also discussed the importance of credit scores, debt management, and the types of insurance and retirement accounts available.

We hope this book has fulfilled its goal of empowering readers with the knowledge and tools to take control of their finances and make informed decisions about their money. Remember, managing your money is a lifelong process, and it is important to continue learning and staying informed about the latest financial trends and practices.

Ultimately, the key to financial success is creating a budget, saving for the future, investing wisely, and protecting your assets. By following these principles, you can achieve your financial goals and build a secure financial future.

So, it is important to remember that managing your finances is not just about making money; it's also about making smart decisions and spending your money wisely. Understanding your income, expenses, and goals can help you make informed decisions about allocating your money.

As you work to improve your financial situation, staying motivated and committed to your goals is also necessary. It may take time and discipline, but the rewards of financial stability and security are well worth the effort.

In conclusion, this book has introduced the basics of money and the tools necessary to take control of your finances and build a secure financial future. Remember to continue learning and staying informed about the latest financial trends and practices, and to remain committed to your financial goals. You can achieve financial success and peace of mind with the proper knowledge and tools.

FIN

ABOUT THE AUTHOR

Yousell Reyes, a native of Puerto Rico, is an accomplished author and translator. He has published several books which aim to empower and inspire individuals to reach their full potential. Additionally, Yousell dedicates a significant amount of time to updating and translating older works, making them more accessible to a modern audience.

As a father of two, Yousell values family time and prioritizes balancing his passion for writing and translating with spending quality time with his loved ones. One of his favorite hobbies is watching movies with his children and enjoying a bowl of popcorn. He believes shared moments with family are crucial for personal growth and development.

Yousell's ultimate goal is to make a positive impact on the lives of others and to help them achieve success in their personal and professional lives. Through his writing and translations, he hopes to empower individuals to believe in themselves and to pursue their dreams.

If you enjoyed this book and received value from it in any way, I would like to ask you a favor: Would you be so kind as to leave a review of this book on Amazon/Kindle? It would be greatly appreciated!

A LITTLE BOOK ABOUT MONEY

NOTES:

Recommended Reading:

"The Total Money Makeover" by Dave Ramsey

"The Total Money Makeover" by Dave Ramsey is a comprehensive guide to personal finance that provides readers with practical steps to take control of their finances. The book emphasizes the importance of living below one's means, avoiding debt, and building wealth through saving and investing. Ramsey's approach to personal finance is based on the idea that individuals can achieve financial freedom by making smart decisions about their money and avoiding common financial pitfalls.

The book is structured as a step-by-step guide, with each chapter focusing on a different aspect of personal finance. The chapters cover topics such as budgeting, saving, investing, paying off debt, and creating a financial plan for the future. Throughout the book, Ramsey provides practical tips and real-life examples to illustrate his financial principles and help readers put them into practice. He also includes motivational anecdotes and encouraging words to keep readers motivated and focused on their financial goals. Whether you're just starting out or looking to improve your financial situation, "The Total Money Makeover" is a comprehensive guide that provides a solid foundation for financial success.

"The Simple Path to Wealth" by JL Collins

"The Simple Path to Wealth" by JL Collins is a comprehensive guide to personal finance and investment strategies. The book is written in a conversational style, making it easy to understand and apply even for those with limited financial knowledge. Collins emphasizes the importance of saving, investing in low-cost index funds, and living below one's means as the key to financial freedom. He also provides insights and lessons learned from his own financial journey, including how he retired at the age of fifty with a significant net worth.

Throughout the book, Collins emphasizes the importance of avoiding consumer debt and focusing on building wealth through investment, rather than trying to get rich quick. He also provides valuable insights into how to prepare for retirement, how to manage risk, and how to deal with market fluctuations. Collins' philosophy is rooted in the idea that slow and steady wins the race when it comes to personal finance and investing. He encourages readers to be patient, disciplined, and focused on the long-term, rather than trying to get rich quick. "The Simple Path to Wealth" is a must-read for anyone looking to take control of their finances and achieve financial freedom.

"**Rich Dad Poor Dad**" by Robert Kiyosaki

"Rich Dad Poor Dad" by Robert Kiyosaki is a personal finance book that aims to challenge traditional thinking about money and wealth. In the book, Kiyosaki shares his own experiences growing up with two father figures, one of whom he calls his "rich dad" who taught him about wealth and finance, and the other he calls his "poor dad" who embodied the traditional 9-5 mentality. Kiyosaki argues that in order to achieve financial independence and true wealth, people must reject the notion that they need a high-paying job and instead learn to invest in assets that generate passive income.

The book is written in a narrative style that makes complex financial concepts accessible and easy to understand. Kiyosaki emphasizes the importance of financial education, risk-taking, and taking control of one's financial future. He covers topics such as real estate investing, starting a business, and the role of taxes in building wealth. The book has been widely popular and has inspired a whole genre of personal finance books that focus on building wealth through alternative means.

"Rich Dad Poor Dad" is a must-read for anyone who wants to re-think their relationship with money and start building a path to financial independence.

"The Psychology of Money" by Morgan Housel

"The Psychology of Money" by Morgan Housel is a unique book that explores the emotional and psychological aspects of money management. It delves into the complex relationships people have with money, and how these relationships influence financial decision-making. The author argues that the way people think and feel about money has a greater impact on their financial success than their actual income or the size of their investment portfolios.

Throughout the book, the author presents real-life stories, examples, and data to illustrate his points. He covers a wide range of topics, including the dangers of overconfidence and the impact of past experiences on financial behavior, the importance of delayed gratification, the psychology of debt and credit, and the role of luck and randomness in financial success. "The Psychology of Money" is a thought-provoking book that offers a fresh perspective on personal finance and provides readers with practical insights into how they can improve their financial lives. It is a must-read for anyone looking to better understand the psychological and emotional factors that drive their financial decisions and behavior.

"I Will Teach You to Be Rich" by Ramit Sethi

"I Will Teach You to Be Rich" is a comprehensive guide to personal finance written by Ramit Sethi. In the book, Sethi provides a step-by-step plan for building wealth and achieving financial freedom. He covers topics ranging from saving and investing to earning more money and managing debt. The book is designed to help readers understand the basics of personal finance, as well as provide practical tips and techniques for achieving financial success.

Sethi approaches personal finance from a unique perspective, focusing on the psychology of money and why people often make poor financial decisions. He stresses the importance of automating savings and investing, and provides advice on how to negotiate salary and start a side hustle to increase income. Throughout the book, Sethi emphasizes the need to make smart financial choices, such as avoiding lifestyle inflation, to achieve long-term financial success. The book also includes actionable exercises and checklists to help readers put the concepts into practice.

www.ingramcontent.com/pod-product-compliance
Lightning Source LLC
Chambersburg PA
CBHW071129240526
45465CB00024B/1550